Blast off!

54321+10

COUNT DOWN

TO YOUR HEALTH!

ACTIVITY BOOK

Live 54321+10™
Numbers to live by!

54321+10® Count Down To Your Health Activity Book is an entertaining way for kids to combine learning with fun while exploring the meaning of each of the count down number themes:

- **5**   Eat 5 fruits and vegetables
- **4**   Drink 4 glasses of water
- **3**   Have 3 good laughs with friends
- **2**   Get 2 hours or less of screen time
- **1**   Get at least 1 hour of physical activity
- **+10**   Get 10 or more hours of sleep

Live 54321+10 is a recommendation for reasonable and achievable lifestyle choices, based on expert advice that kids can make each day to stay healthy. The six themes, represented by each of the numbers in the title, remind kids of simple habits to guide them to better health.

Blast off!

EAT MORE FRUITS & VEGETABLES

Challenge a Friend

Compare your answers with a friend. Cross off any answers you had that were the same. The person with the most answers left wins!

a.

b.

c.

*D.

E.

f.

g.

*H.

*i.

*J.

k.

L.

m.

*n.

O.

P.

*Q.

R.

s.

T.

*u.

*V.

w.

*X.

Y.

z.

©Learning ZoneXpress

ALPHABET SALAD

Parker Pepper is trying to think of a fruit or vegetable for each letter of the alphabet.

Can you help him?

Give yourself one point for each fruit or vegetable you can list under the correct letter. Give yourself two points if you can name a fruit or vegetable for the letters that have a star by them.

WHiCH iS WHiCH

Buddy Broccoli loves to go to the Farmers Market in his community. Today he has two shopping baskets—one for fruits and one for vegetables.

Draw a circle around the foods that should go in his fruit basket. Draw a box around the foods that should go in his vegetables basket.

(Draw your favorite fruit here.)

(Draw your favorite vegetable here.)

©Learning ZoneXpress

DiD You KNOW?

The oldest Farmers Market still in operation in the U.S. is Lancaster, Pennsylvania's Central Market. People have been buying fresh fruits and vegetables there since 1730!

Fruit Hunt

Maya Mango and her friend Brianna Banana are touring the community garden in their neighborhood. Their goal is to find and name as many fruits as they can.

Help them search by circling the names of fruits in the word find to the right. Names are hidden up, down, forward, backward, or diagonal.

How many did you find?

```
E O G N A M S A H J G A M J W
R G L Q A U T Y S H N E W V X
A W N V H A R A P A L I Y I P
R P E A C H A P N O M Y W I Q
E U P X R J W A N N L U N I E
Y A W L V O B P K Q M E X N K
K C S T E A E K K U A O D R E
Y R R E H C R M N P C C C O M
T B C T N F R L P G P T R B B
N C S O Y K I L P R B J K V O
E C M T Q W E E A A Z Z U N U
R P W U Y G S P O P B V G T D
W P N V E Y B N H E B O R U W
L I I X M Z I P T O P Z I Y K
T L K V K Z L C S Z X N J R H
```

WHAT'S

Pedro Potato is trying to help his family get a serving of vegetables at every meal. He took a look at the menu for the next three days and saw that no vegetables were included!

Help Pedro Potato think of a tasty vegetable to include with each meal to make it complete. His goal is a colorful plate!

Draw or write your answer in the space provided.

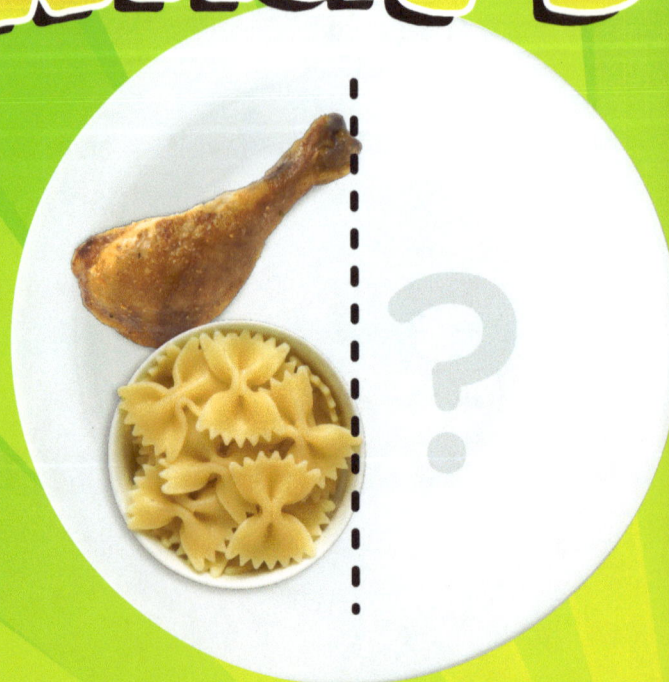

Draw a picture of your favorite fruit.

WORD BANK

peach   grape
cherry   apple
orange   pineapple
strawberries   kiwi
banana   melon
papaya   mango

BONUS QUESTION

Where does your favorite fruit grow?
(example: on a tree, bush, plant, etc.)

MISSING?

MARVELOUS MAZE

Carrie Carrot is on a mission to get all the carrots picked and hauled from one end of the garden to the basket at the other end. Help her find her way and see how many carrots you can get to the basket.

FINISH

START

Fruit & Veggie Tic-Tac-Toe

X O X O X

Cody Cauliflower has challenged his friend Sammy Squash to a game of Fruit and Veggie Tic-Tac-Toe. Cody draws a cauliflower in the square when it is his turn. Sammy draws a squash in the square when it is his turn. Help them finish the game. Who got three in a row first?

Eat A Rainbow

Wanda Watermelon loves art. She has drawn a rainbow and wants to fill it in with fruits and vegetables that match each color. Can you help her? Draw in as many fruits and vegetables as you can think of to match each color.

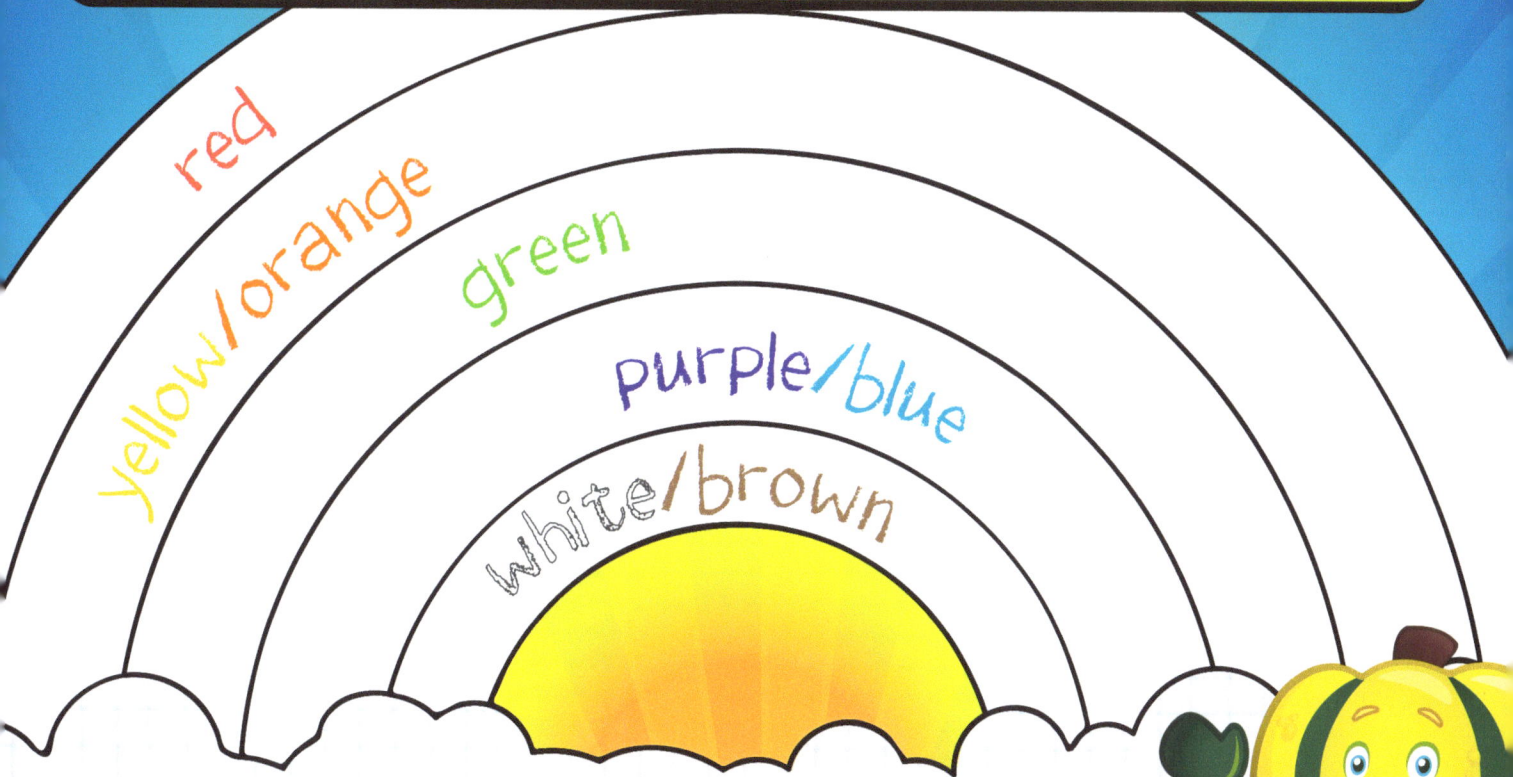

red

yellow/orange

green

purple/blue

white/brown

Partner up with a friend and play a game of Fruit and Veggie Tic-Tac-Toe. Choose which fruits or vegetables you will draw. The first person to get three in a row wins.

Favorites Countdown

You've helped the Garden Heroes learn more about fruits and vegetables. Now it's time to count down with your favorites! Write or draw your answers to each of the questions below.

5 My favorite fruit to eat for a snack is _____

4 My favorite vegetable to eat for breakfast is _____

3 My favorite fruit to eat on a warm day is _____

2 My favorite vegetable to eat on a pizza is _____

1 My favorite vegetable or fruit to grow in a garden is _____

Blast off!

DRINK MORE WATER

Help Wanda search for tasty things to add to her water.
Look up, down, forward, backward, and on the diagonal to find the hidden words.

WORD BANK

lime slices
lemon juice
frozen mango
raspberry

mint
basil leaves
cucumber
thyme

```
O L Y R R E B P S A R D X F L
B Z F W D A S P J K U L E S I
K A A W K B Z O A Q E K G J M
R K S F R O Z E N M A N G O E
Y E F I Y R H V O M C D F U S
B V B S L T U N O X X Y E G L
R R I M N L J B O H W M M C I
S F Q I U U E S Z O O M E L C
O P M U I C D A J X Y E R A E
K M B C Y T U I V G M M B U S
T K E D N I V C O E I Y W L L
T P T H E P V W A N S H F U K
J Z V O Y C B L D G O T H S N
C U D R M H Z M L I D K V K U
I R X C A C P P E W V O I O Q
```

©Learning ZoneXpress

Wanda Watermelon sometimes has a hard time choosing water to drink because she thinks it's too boring. There are lots of ways to jazz up your water and still keep it healthy. Some people add natural flavors to water to help them drink more of it.

FLAVOR It!

Can you think of some tasty things to add to your water?

1.

2.

3.

4.

Try spicing up your water by adding sliced jalapeño peppers. **SPICY!**

CRAZY FLAVORS!

Selling a Splash

Summertime is a great time to set up a lemonade stand...but water would be a healthier choice for everyone. Help Gordon Grape design a water stand where he can sell water to his thirsty friends and neighbors. Design a creative sign and menu on the water stand below.

What should he name his water stand?

Should he add any fruits or flavors to the water?

How much should he charge?

©Learning ZoneXpress

What will be on his menu?

WATER WORDS

Andi Apple and Sammy Squash love to run through the sprinkler. Color blue over the words in the picture that have to do with water.

breeze
river
leaf
paint
spray
soak
flowers
hose
drizzle
drink
summer
sea
H2O

©Learning ZoneXpress

Chart it!

Join Olivia Orange in her quest to track how much water she drinks. Color in one glass on the chart for each glass of water you drink each day. Try for four glasses every day.

gulp   clouds   aquatic   horse

sun   play

marine   gym   rainwater

dampen   grass   drip

eat   wet

Water Facts

Help Andi Apple and Sammy Squash find the facts! Complete the following sentences with words from the word bank.

1. You can live 3 to 5 _ _ _ _ without water.

2. Drink_ _ _ _ glasses of _ _ _ _ _ _ each day.

3. You_ _ _ _ water when you sweat, so make sure to drink water after activities.

4. All _ _ _ _ _ _ _ things need water to survive.

5. Water helps us digest _ _ _ _ _ .

6. Water helps flush _ _ _ _ _ _ from the body.

7. More than _ _ _ _ _ of your body is made up of water.

8. If your mouth is _ _ _ _, you probably need to drink more water.

WORD BANK

lose
living
four
food
days
water
dry
half
waste

©Learning ZoneXpress

Today Olivia Drank:	Day 1 I drank:	Day 2 I drank:	Day 3 I drank:	Day 4 I drank:	Day 5 I drank:

Smart Drink Choices

There are lots of ways to get enough water. There is water in every beverage we drink and in the foods we eat—especially fruits and vegetables.

Brianna Banana knows just how important water is for the body. She wants to make sure she is drinking the healthiest beverages possible to get lots of water and avoid extra calories, sugar, and caffeine.

Help Brianna Banana make a good drink choice by circling the healthiest beverages in her refrigerator.

Trivia

Which state in the United States has the most lakes?

Answer: Alaska

©Learning ZoneXpress

Fun Fact

Dehydration (De-hy-dra-tion) is something that happens to your body when you don't get enough water.

How do you feel when you are dehydrated? Circle all the correct answers.

a. tired

b. cranky

c. energized

d. unable to concentrate

e. dizzy

How did you feel when you have been dehydrated?

_____

_____

Answer: a, b, d

Why I think water is the best drink choice...

1.

2.

3.

WHY WATER

Spencer Spinach is doing a report at school on water. He has to list three reasons why water is the best drink choice anyone can make.

Can you help him?
List the reasons above.

FAVORITES COUNTDOWN

You've helped the Garden Heroes learn more about water. Now it's time to count down with your favorites! Write or draw your answers to each of the questions below.

5 My favorite way to drink water is

4 My favorite time to drink water is

3 My favorite cup or bottle to drink water from is

2 My favorite fruit to add to water is

1 My favorite place to drink water is

Blast off!

ANSWERS FOR PAGE 17: 1) days, 2) four, water, 3) lose, 4) living, 5) food, 6) waste, 7) half, 8) dry

ANSWERS FOR PAGE 14

LAUGH MORE

WRANGLE WORRY

Spencer Spinach is doing a school report on worry. He has learned that worry is something you feel when you are nervous, uncomfortable, or overwhelmed. Worrying can make you feel angry, afraid, or even sick!

Can you help me find ways to reduce worry in the word search below?

Rememeber to search up, down, forward, backward, and on the diagonal to find the hidden words.

```
Q Z S Y C J G X V M U Q P X W
X U D E R O H V R V P L K U G
I N U M E C O Q O Z A N F C T
F I N R N E Q K A Y Y M R N C
J D B Z C M T U D B D G G U B
L C B N U T S W Y T K U J I R
H G A A W D S U G H N T K W X
E D M T J W H L H Q X I T G J
J S Q R C H T U X L E O N E U
O D I N U R A L T S T V F L N
C Z P C F P L W T I O B G A M
I Q W N R D K O Q S K N S W A
S Q U R N E P T L A U G H M K
U F H V Q X X F F I R Q B R E
M Q A G D Y P E H C F R N C F
```

WORD BANK

music	cook	talk
dance	run	cry
laugh	play	exercise

©Learning ZoneXpress

DID YOU KNOW

Most people can't laugh on command.

The sound of laughter is a universal language.

One good belly laugh burns about 35 calories.

Wipe Out Worry

Craven Corn is learning to deal with stress by identifying the things that he worries about and brainstorming what he can do to wipe out worry from his life. Now it's your turn! Fill in the chart below.

TRY THIS

Next time one of these things listed below causes you worry, try the suggestion you came up with and see if it helps.

©Learning ZoneXpress

	How often does this cause you worry?	How can you deal with the worry?
my parents' problems		
my homework		
not enough time to play		
arguments with friends or siblings		
someone I know who is sick		
not getting enough sleep		
have too many things to do		
scary weather		
team competition		

Olivia Orange just learned what a hyperbole is.

Do you know what it is?

A hyperbole (pronounced hi-PER-bowl-ee) is emphasizing something by using exaggeration.

Here is an example of a hyperbole that Olivia wrote:

One summer it was so hot that all the flowers grew upside down to stay cool, and even the sun had to install an air conditioner!

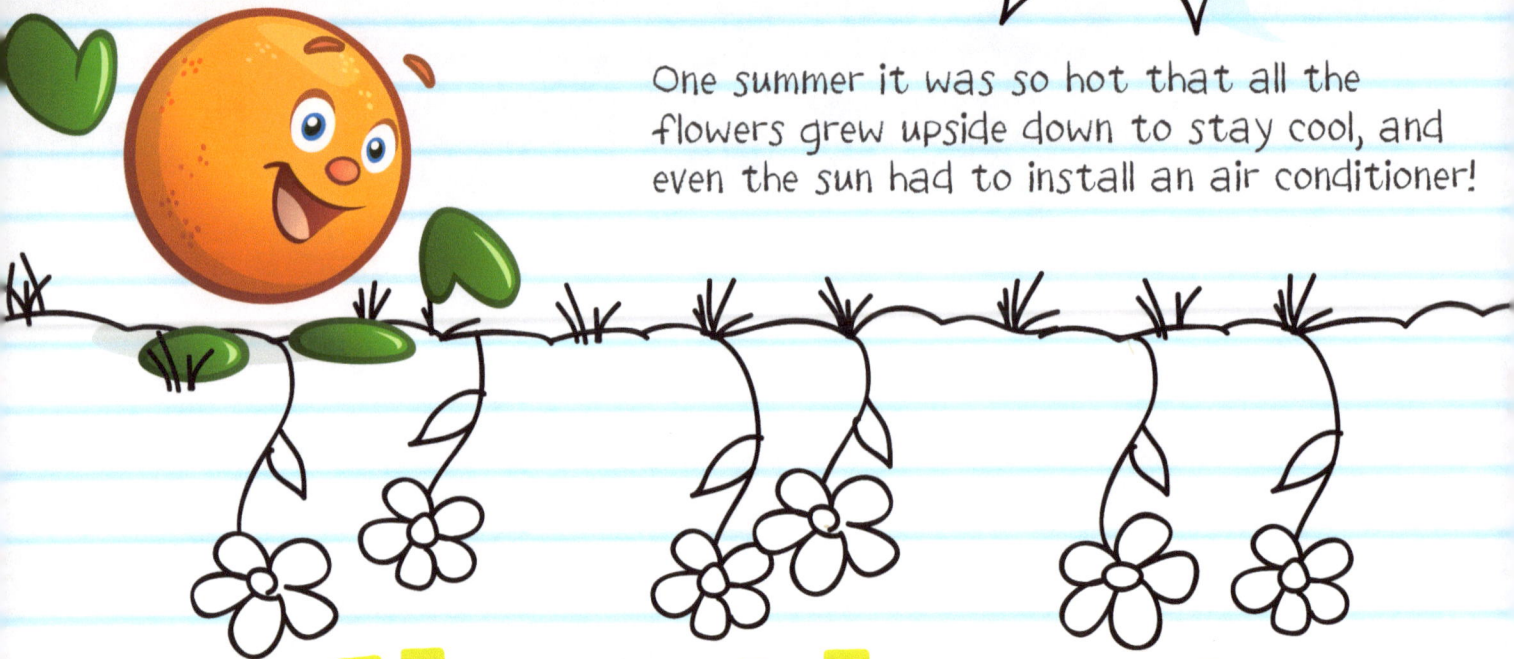

Hilarious Hyperbole

Hyperboles can be very funny. Write your own by finishing the sentences below.

1. My room is so messy that...

2. Last night it rained so much that...

LAUGH YOUR HEAD OFF

Callie Cabbage and Pepe Pineapple love to laugh. Just the other day, they laughed so hard that they started to cry!

When is the last time you laughed so hard your stomach hurt or you could hardly breathe?

In the space below, draw a picture of what happened.

(Draw your picture here.)

CRACK the CODE

Kimi Kiwi knows it is very important to take care of herself but sometimes she feels worried and does not know what to do to make things better.

Below are several ideas for how she can keep herself calm. Can you help Kimi by decoding the message?

CODE KEY

t = ◗	c = ◉
p = ✖	v = ◀
a = ◇	L = ↑
r = ϟ	e = ▲
h = →	f = ♎
y = ○	n = ★
k = ↙	g = ✪
s = ▶	j = ◁
i = ✳	o = ↗
y = ⬤	u = ▼
d = ❖	w = 💧

W O R R Y can make us feel tired, scared,

or sad. When we are **W O R R I E D**,

it is good to **T A L K** to someone we trust.

Sometimes sharing **F E E L I N G S** can

make the worry go away. **L A U G H T E R**

is one **H E A L T H Y** way to deal with worry.

Laughter makes us feel light and full of **J O Y**.

P H Y S I C A L

A C T I V I T Y is another good way to

deal with our worries.

PLAY AND RELAX

When he feels worried, Pedro Potato likes to play catch or bike. When CeCe Cantaloupe is worried, she likes to relax in her hammock. Playing and relaxing are two of the best things you can do when you are worried about something.

Write or draw your favorite ways to play and relax in the space below.

Ways I like to play...

Ways I like to relax...

Blast Off with Laughter

Billy Blueberry is counting down with his favorite jokes. See if you can complete each joke by combining the questions with the correct answers.

5 Why did the bacon laugh? _____

4 What's the strongest vegetable in the world? _____

3 Why did the banana peel? _____

2 What has four legs and can't walk? _____

1 What side of a chicken has the most feathers? _____

Blast off!

Now, blast off into laughter by writing your own joke for Billy's list.

_____
_____
_____
_____

ANSWER KEY

It wasn't wearing sunscreen.

A table.   The outside.

Because the egg cracked a yolk.

The muscle sprout.

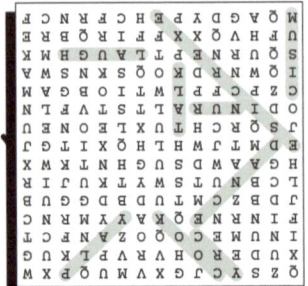

Less Screen Time

SCREENS EVERYWHERE

Buddy Broccoli wants to do a screen scavenger hunt in his living room. Help him find all the devices with screens that his family has in their living room.

Do you think your family has this many screens or more in your house?

©Learning ZoneXpress

	Total screen time	How did I spend my screen time?	Did I get less than 2 hours of screen time? (not including homework)
Example	3	1 hour on Facebook 1 hour watching part of a movie 1 hour playing video games	No!
MONDAY			
TUESDAY			
WEDNESDAY			
THURSDAY			
FRIDAY			

Track It!

After locating all the screens in his living room, Buddy Broccoli decided to keep track of his screen time for one week. He discovered that he was spending too much time in front of screens.

How do you think your screen time stacks up?

Use the chart above to track your screen time for one week.

DARE DECODE

CODE KEY

a = ◗   y = ◉
c = ◇   t = ◀
h = ↑   m = ⚡
l = ↙   i = ▲
n = ✖   d = ♎
g = →   s = ★
e = ○   r = ✪
u = ▶   v = ◁
o = ✱   k = ↗
        w = ▷

I have a screen time challenge for you! Decode the dare by using the code key above.

Here's a **challenge** for **you**:
◇ ↑ ◗ ↙ ↙ ○ ✖ → ○   ◉ ✱ ▶

Spend the same **amount** of **time**
◗ ⚡ ✱ ▶ ✖ ◀   ◀ ▲ ⚡ ○

you spend each **day** in front of a
♎ ◗ ◉

screen being physically
★ ◇ ✪ ○ ○ ✖

active. Can **you** do it? What about
◗ ◇ ◀ ▲ ◁ ○   ◉ ✱ ▶

this challenge – **could** you spend an
◇ ✱ ▶ ↙ ♎

entire **weekend**
○ ✖ ◀ ▲ ✪ ○   ▷ ○ ○ ↗ ○ ✖ ♎

with no **screen** time? Try it!
★ ◇ ✪ ○ ○ ✖

Answers to page 33:
1) adults, 2) commercials, 3) bedrooms, 4) eat, 5) off, 6) music

Draw a picture of your favorite activity that does not involve using a screen.

Screen Time
Word Search & Tips

Help Kimi Kiwi complete these screen time suggestions by filling in the blanks. Complete the following tips with words from the Word Bank.

1. Have TV time rules for the kids and the

_____ in a family.

2. Do something else when _____ come on.

3. Don't have TVs in the _____.

4. Don't watch TV while you _____.

5. Decide what show you are going to watch. After

you watch it, turn the TV _____.

6. If you want background sound, listen to _____.

Word Bank

off
eat
bedrooms
commercials
music
adults

©Learning ZoneXpress

Billy Blueberry is searching for the health risks that are associated with too much screen time.

Can you help him?

Find and circle the words from the word bank below. Look up, down, forward, backward, and on the diagonal.

```
O O J S E V R J T V P D B E Y
C N A Y R K C A B U M E R K N
S L I N U S W M A B J A H Y B
I N A Z T I J R G Z D S F M D
T I R C S J A T I E U T R V L
M X L W O I H E L S R X S B O
I K G F P G X J S D T K G D X
L I P P I C J Q M W B W A R P
P A J E S L E E P E N K C E J
R N W O M R U X B Y L B C M M
B A T R S S B E Q E J R J E Z
X R B C C T D H Q S E T T M N
I Z B B F F W K E R W O O M T
X U V Q P E Q P A D F O T A C
V V I P H M F P N M D K V T L
```

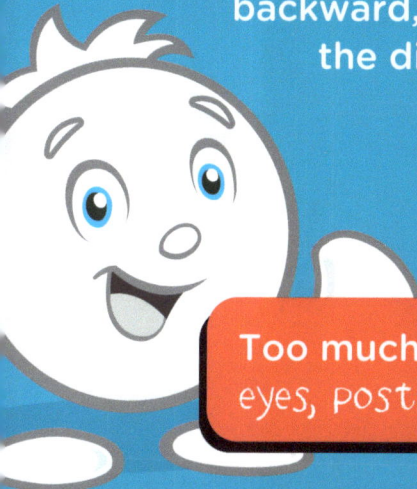

Too much screen time can be bad for your:
eyes, posture, weight, mood, sleep, wrist, back, neck

Word Bank

SCREEN SAVER

Sadie Sweet Potato does not want to be a couch potato, but needs some helpful reminders to step away from the screen. Draw a screen saver that shows fun activities that do not need a screen.

(Quiz Answers: 1. D; 2. A, C, D; 3. A, B; 4. C)

Quiz Me

April Asparagus is trying to complete a quiz on the effects of screen time. Do you think you know the answers? Circle all the correct answers.

1. Too much screen time is linked to

    A. depression   B. obesity

    C. sleep problems   D. all of the above

2. What counts as screen time?

    A. time watching TV

    B. time doing homework on a computer

    C. time playing video games

    D. time texting

3. Too much screen time can

    A. give you a headache

    B. make you feel tired

    C. give you energy

    D. help you learn

4. Experts say kids should get less than ____ hours of screen time each day.

    A. 3   B. 4

    C. 2   D. 10

Survey Says

Parker Pepper knows it's not just kids who should limit their screen time—adults should too! Parker is pretending he is a reporter for the school newspaper and will inverview his dad using the survey below. Now it's your turn to be the reporter! Use Parker's survey below to find out how much screen time one of your relatives gets each day.

Relative's Name: Age:

How many hours do you spend in front of a screen each day?

Do you watch TV while you eat?

Do you have a TV or computer in your bedroom?

How soon after you wake up do you check your smartphone?

Do you use a computer for work?

Do you think you should have less screen time?

Are there things you want to get done that you don't because of your screen time?

Have you had any injuries from working at a computer?

©Learning ZoneXpress

Were you surprised by the results?
----
yes or no

Here's a CHALLENGE for YOU: Spend the same AMOUNT of TIME you spend each DAY in front of a SCREEN being physically ACTIVE. Can YOU do it? What about this challenge - COULD you spend an ENTIRE WEEKEND with no SCREEN time? Try it!

Answers to page 32 Decode Dare:

INSTEAD OF... COUNTDOWN

You've helped the Garden Heroes learn more about how to have less screen time. Now it's time to count down! Write or draw your answers to each of the sentences below.

5 Instead of watching TV, I could _____

4 Instead of playing video games, I could _____

3 Instead of texting with friends, I could _____

2 Instead of watching movies, I could _____

1 Instead of being on the Internet, I could _____

Blast off!

ANSWERS FOR PAGE 33

MORE PHYSICAL ACTIVITY

Sleep Tips Decoded

Sarah Snap Pea's list of things that will help her fall asleep has been put into code. Oh no!

Can you help her by decoding the list below?

1. Take a warm _____ before bed.
   ❖ ◇ ◗ → (bath)

2. Go to sleep when you feel _____.
   ■ ⚡ ↗ ∩ ▶ ● (drowsy)

3. Listen to soft and relaxing _____.
   ◁ ▼ ▶ ✳ ▷ (music)

4. Sleep in a _____ room.
   ■ ◇ ⚡ ↙ (dark)

5. Get _____ hours of sleep a night!
   ◗ ▲ ★ (ten)

6. Don't watch _____ before bed.
   ◗ ▲ ↑ ▲ ◀ ✳ ▶ ✳ ↗ ★ (television)

7. Don't be on the _____ before bed.
   ▷ ↗ ◁ ✖ ▼ ◗ ▲ ⚡ (computer)

8. Don't eat anything with _____ before bedtime.
   ▶ ▼ ↺ ◇ ⚡ (sugar)

9. Don't drink anything with _____ before bedtime.
   ▷ ◇ ✪ ✪ ▲ ✳ ★ ▲ (caffeine)

Code Key

g = ↺	m = ◁	L = ↑	t = ◗	c = ▷	h = →	u = ▼
k = ↙	s = ▶	o = ↗	e = ▲	p = ✖	v = ◀	y = ○	d = ■
w = ∩	b = ❖	n = ★	f = ✪	a = ◇	r = ⚡	i = ✳	y = ●

Bedtime Snacks

Tommy Tomato loves a bedtime snack. He knows it's important to choose healthy snacks that help him sleep—not unhealthy ones that could keep him awake.

Do you know what to eat before bed that won't get in the way of a good night's sleep?

Put a circle around the foods that are good choices before bed. Put an X through the foods that are not a good choice before bed.

What is your favorite healthy bedtime snack? Draw a picture of it here.

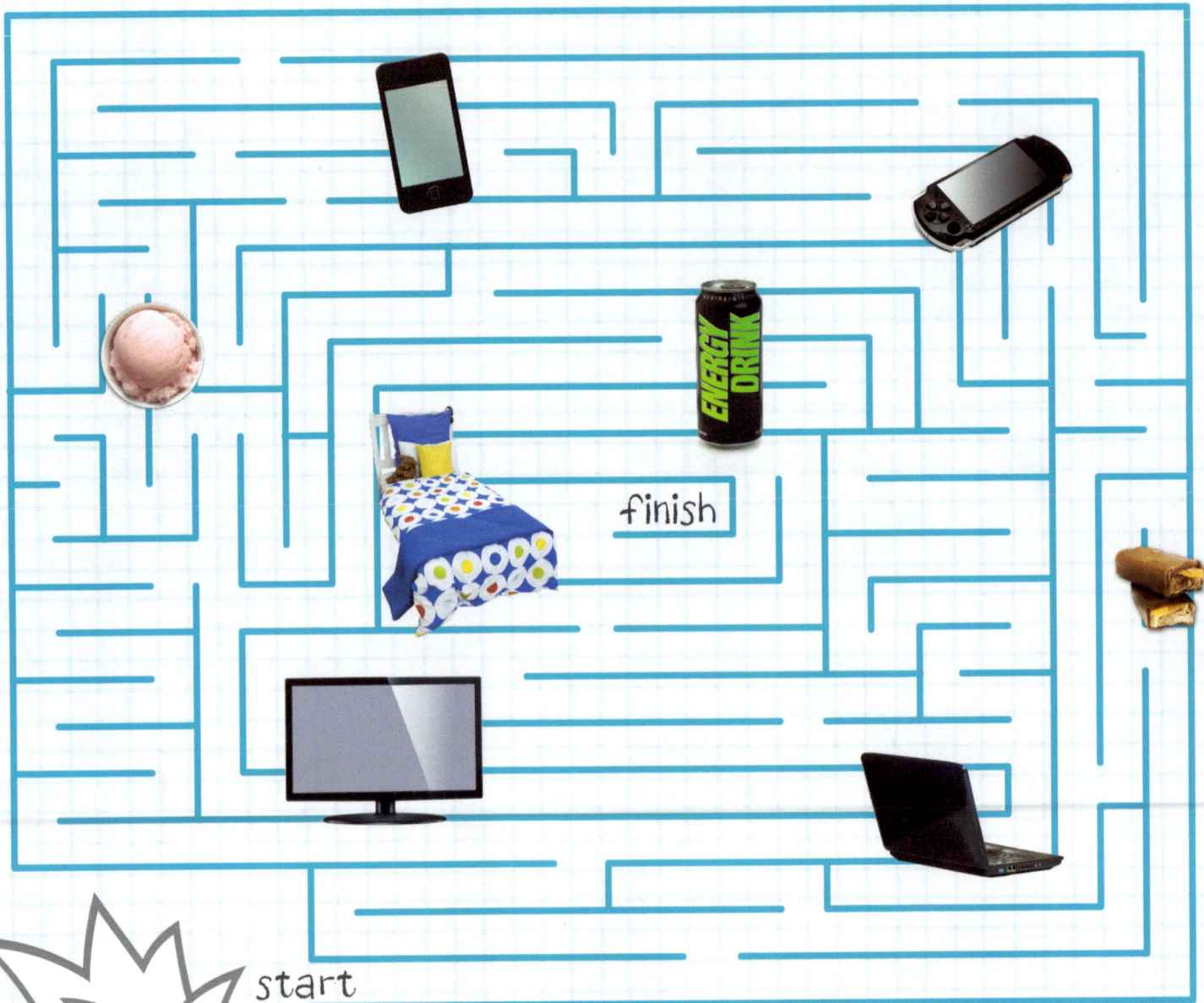

finish

start

Sleep Walk

Help Pepe Pineapple navigate his way past some common roadblocks to sleep so he can get a good night of rest and feel energized for the next day.

Do any of these roadblocks ever get in your way of a good night's sleep? What can you do to change that?

SCHEDULE YOUR SLEEP

Look at the bedtimes of the Garden Heroes below. Draw in the hands on the clock to show when each Hero will wake up if he or she gets 10 hours of sleep.

NOW IT'S YOUR TURN!

Draw in the hands on the clocks for when you go to bed and wake up each day for four days.

Did you get at least 10 hours?

	Went to bed	Woke up	
APRIL 			
PEDRO 			
BRIANNA 			
STELLA 			

Went to bed	Woke up	
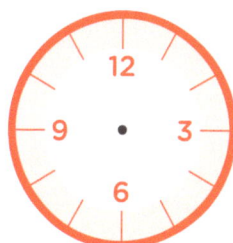		**DAY 1** ☐ YES ☐ NO
		**DAY 2** ☐ YES ☐ NO
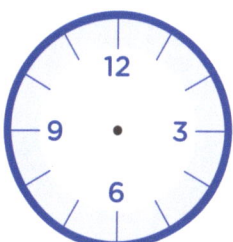	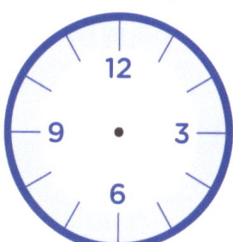	**DAY 3** ☐ YES ☐ NO
		**DAY 4** ☐ YES ☐ NO

©Learning ZoneXpress

41

WHAT'S THE PROBLEM?

Mo Mushroom goes to bed at 7:30, but he can't fall asleep. Look at the picture of Mo's room. Draw an X through the things that should be removed from his room to help him fall asleep more easily.

Giraffes are the mammals that get the least amount of sleep—less than 2 hours each day!

Koalas are the mammals that sleep the most. They sleep 22 hours a day.

Sleepy Time

Now you know a lot of things that you can do to help you get a good night of sleep. Circle the sleep tips in the word find below. Remember to search up, down, forward, backward, and on the diagonal to find the hidden words.

WORD BANK

drink milk   soft music

quiet room   dark room

read a book

What will help me get a good night's sleep? Can you help me find the tips?

```
Q J F N G N B W D Z S K D I Z
R U B H N C A B U N L O A X J
R S I A H R N S Q I X O R O D
Z K X E M Z B L M Z H B K V D
F B L B T V A K I U M A R A P
M G A L L R N U C W L D O A X
E T J B U I O T J H M A O V Y
H O F J R L P O O Z O E M N A
A N T D F C U A M U T R W Q L
S O F T M U S I C N Q G D B N
N R M H H L H W V J E M M G G
C K J N Z V Y O T D M N G S X
H E M A X R F J I D U E L J T
S C B B R Q J K B S V G C B L
P Q V E U O Y J M N Y A E C S
```

©Learning ZoneXpress

Kids should get 10 hours of sleep each night. How much sleep do you usually get?

Glue a picture of yourself here.

Favorites Countdown

You've helped the Garden Heroes learn more about physical activity. Now it's time to count down with your favorites! Write or draw your answers to each of the questions below.

5 My favorite type of physical activity to do by myself is _____

4 My favorite type of physical activity to do with a friend is _____

3 My favorite type of physical activity to do outdoors is _____

2 My favorite type of physical activity to do indoors is _____

1 My favorite type of physical activity that gets me messy and dirty is _____

Blast off!

MORE SLEEP

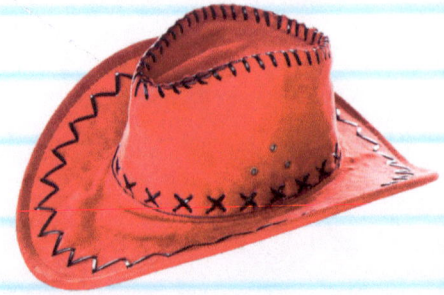

ACTIVE ANDI

Andi Apple is looking for new ways to be physically active. Above are different objects that she found around her house. Look at the objects and give Andi ideas about how she can get active!

My Ideas for Andi...

1. Example: Andi could put her dog on the leash and take him on a walk.

2.

3.

4.

5.

6.

Track It

Gordon Grape decided to keep track of his physical activity for 3 days. His goal was to do one hour of physical activity each day. Look at his results and color in the clocks to show how many minutes he was active.

Day	Physical Activity	Number of Minutes	Did he make his goal?	How many more minutes did he need?
Monday	Rode bike for 30 minutes	(clock)	no	(clock)
Tuesday	Jumped rope for 15 minutes	(clock)		(clock)
Wednesday	Went swimming for 60 minutes	(clock)		(clock)

Now It's Your Turn!

Record your physical activity for the next 3 days. Are you getting enough?

Day	Physical Activity	Number of Minutes	Did you make your goal?	How many more minutes did you need?
		(clock)		(clock)
		(clock)		(clock)
		(clock)		(clock)

Get MOVING!

Sadie Sweet Potato knows that she needs to increase her physical activity. Read below about Sadie's day. Help her think of ways she could be more active. Write or draw your ideas in the space provided.

Sadie rides in a car to school.

Sadie could _____ to school.

1.

©Learning ZoneXpress

WHAT COUNTS?

April Asparagus is trying to figure out which of her favorite things count as physical activities. Can you help her? Circle the things on April's list that you think are physical activities.

Can you think of 5 more things that count as physical activity? Write them in to add to April's list.

48

Sadie sits on a bench with a friend at recess.

Sadie could _____ at recess.

2.

Sadie watches television after homework.

Sadie could _____ after homework.

3.

skateboarding

drawing a picture

hockey

running

baseball

bike riding

swimming

sleeping

reading a book

basketball

walking in the grocery store

cleaning the bathroom

taking the dog on a hike

playing a video game

reading a book

gardening

raking leaves

canoeing

dancing

TRUE OR FALSE:

Staring at a blank wall burns more calories than watching TV.

Answer: True!

Activities Scramble

Olivia Orange and her friends can't decide what to do.
Help Olivia unscramble the sports below and then color
in the star next to the activity that you think she
and her friends should try first.

1. snniet

2. gniabrotskade

3. lketablbas

4. sabeball

5. cie ingkats

6. balltfos

7. ginbki

8. reccos

9. llbatfoo

10. mmswngii

Oh no! The benefits of staying active have gone missing!

Help Spencer Spinach find them. Search up, down, forward, backward, and on the diagonal to find the hidden words. Then use the same words to complete the sentences below. Put a star next to the benefit that you think is the most important.

```
T K F I N N D C P I X O J S U
L G N W U S T N T E Q G V E P
S K Q S X E H S F T I R O N L
N S W J S H C T R G F E V O M
V K P R L C Q W H B M A F B S
E W B T E O C G U G D Q U D X
H N T W E W N O R B I N N N K
C M O K P V H G I B M E O A X
E W U Q C U C L E N I H W S K
L I W A Z S Z G X R N B R E W
A L B F R U J R F J O W X L R
Y W P R X J L S L Y X O I C J
Q U U U P O O O E H J L U S X
K S F I E P D X O H T M F U S
Q J Z A D A Y W S H I I R M Q
```

Stay Active

WORD BANK

weight
sleep
longer
fun
move
muscles and bones
friends

Benefits:

1. Physical activity increases your chances of living __ __ __ __ __ __.

2. Physical activity helps you __ __ __ __ __ better at night.

3. As you get older, physical activity will help you

   __ __ __ __ around more easily.

4. Physical activity helps you have stronger

   __.

5. Physical activity helps you keep a healthy __ __ __ __ __ __.

6. Physical activity allows you to be with __ __ __ __ __ __ __.

7. Physical activity is __ __ __!

©Learning ZoneXpress

COUNT DOWN TO A GREAT NIGHT'S SLEEP

Help Gracie Grapefruit get ready to blast off into a great night of sleep by putting the steps of her bedtime routine into the order that you think makes the most sense.

Draw a line from the bedtime step to the number. Remember, you're counting backwards, so make the first activity #5, and go down to #1 as the last activity!

5

4

3

2

1

Climb into bed and turn out the lights.

Read a story.

Brush teeth.

Take a warm bath.

Eat a healthy snack.

Blast off to a great night's sleep!

Blast off!